Tessellations Everywhere

By Susan Schott Karr

CELEBRATION PRESS
Pearson Learning Group

Contents

Patterns Around the World

Throughout history, people have used patterns to add beauty to the world around them. The Japanese made patterns when they carved wooden screens. The Navajo made patterns when they wove rugs. In Spain, bright **tiles** were used when walls inside a castle were designed. People in different parts of the world have used **mosaic** designs in making walls, floors, and windows for hundreds of years.

Sometimes people use a special kind of pattern in making things. These special patterns are called tessellations (tess-uh-LAY-shunz). This book will tell you more about tessellations. You'll also learn why tessellations can be fun.

Tiles on the Blue Mosque in Afghanistan make colorful patterns.

3

What Is a Tessellation?

A tessellation is a shape that repeats itself. As the shape repeats, it fills the surface without any **gaps**. The shapes don't **overlap**. A tessellation is like a puzzle. All of the pieces must fit together. The sides of each shape touch, making a pattern that can go on forever.

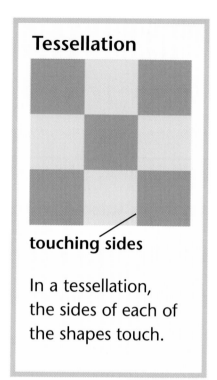

Tessellation

touching sides

In a tessellation, the sides of each of the shapes touch.

a Roman mosaic showing a dog on a leash

The word *tessellation* comes from *tessella*. This ancient Roman term means "square tile." Years ago, the Romans used small square tiles to create mosaics. When shapes in a design repeat to make a tessellation, we say that they tessellate.

Shapes That Work

The shapes that can be used to create tessellations must be the same size. What type of shapes can people use to create tessellations? Squares, triangles, and hexagons work. These shapes are all **polygons**. They are made of three or more straight sides. The sides of these polygons are equal in length. The squares, triangles, or hexagons that can be put together in a tessellation are **congruent**. That means they are the same shape and size.

These three polygons can form tessellations.	These shapes tessellate.
triangle: three sides 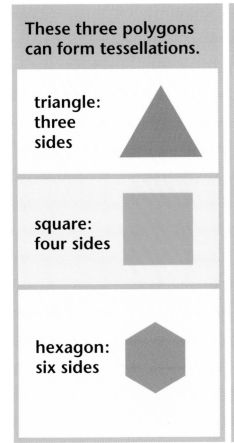	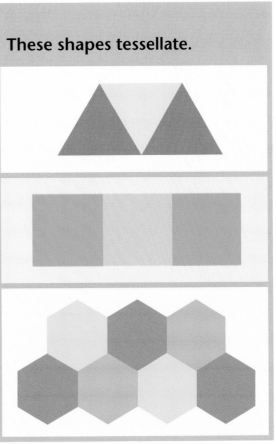
square: four sides	
hexagon: six sides	

Shapes That Don't Work

Not all shapes can be used to make tessellations. In general, only polygons with three, four, or six sides will create a pattern that tessellates.

Circles don't work. When you cover a surface with circles that touch, there are gaps between the circles. Octagons, or eight-sided figures, also don't work. You could not make a tessellation using stop signs, which have eight sides. There would be gaps between the signs.

Circles leave gaps. They do not tessellate.

Octagons leave gaps. They do not tessellate.

Tessellating Tiles

A tile is a **unit** that repeats to make a pattern. You can think of it as one piece of a puzzle. The tile may be as simple as a single square. However, more than one shape can be put together to form a tile. For example, two triangles or four squares can be fit together to make a tile. The shapes in the tile do not overlap.

After the smaller pieces are fit together to create a tile, the whole tile is repeated to form a pattern. These units must also fit together without gaps or overlaps. There are different ways the tiles can be used to make tessellations.

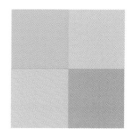

These four squares fit together to make a tile.

These two triangles fit together to make a tile.

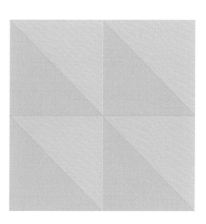

repeating tiles

Tessellations That Line Up

The tile may repeat side by side to form a pattern that goes in one direction. The result is one row of shapes that repeat. For example, a sidewalk can be a row of squares.

However, the tile can also be repeated on a surface in all directions. Then there is more than one row of tiles.

In this tessellation, the sidewalk squares line up in one row.

In this tessellation, the shapes repeat in all directions.

Color and Shading

Color choices can make tessellations look bright or dull. What happens if the tiles you tessellate are all red? You would see just a plain red surface. How can you come up with an interesting pattern? Using different colors, or **shades** of the same color, make the tiles stand out.

How many colors do you need to use to see the tessellations? With triangles and squares, you need two colors. However, with hexagons, you need three. Otherwise, hexagons next to each other will be the same color. One hexagon will blend into the next. Color and shading make tessellations fun to look at.

two colors for tessellating triangles

two colors for tessellating squares

three colors for tessellating hexagons

making a tessellation with different colored tiles

swimming pool with
tessellating tiles

Tessellations in Everyday Life

Not only are tessellations found all around the world, they may be right in front of you, below your feet, or over your head. They may be right inside your own home. The beautiful patterns made by tessellations can be found in bathroom and kitchen tiles, brick paths, and wallpaper.

Tessellations may be found in nature, too. A honeycomb is a tessellating pattern made by bees. Look at a slice of a honeycomb, and you will see congruent hexagons. They repeat in all directions.

The Giant's Causeway in Ireland is made up of tessellating hexagonal columns. They are the result of a volcanic eruption millions of years ago.

Symmetry

Every tessellation has **symmetry**. A figure has line symmetry if it can be folded along a line so that both parts match exactly.

Symmetry is all around us. For example, the wings of a butterfly **mirror** each other. The reflection of a landscape in water shows symmetry.

symmetry in nature

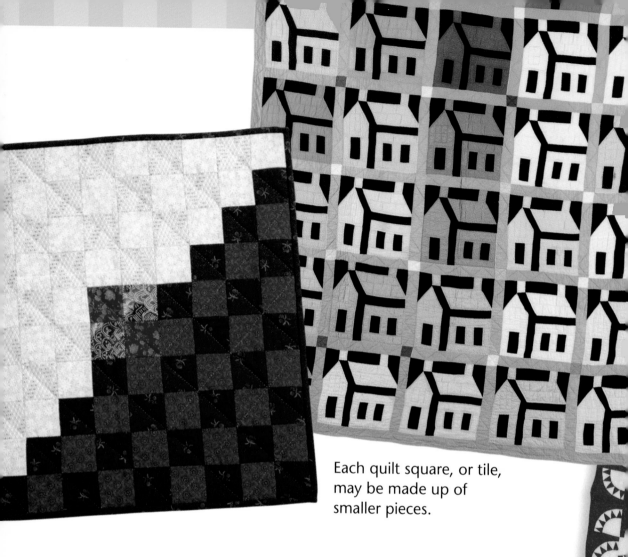

Each quilt square, or tile, may be made up of smaller pieces.

For **centuries**, people have used symmetry to make quilts. Quilters have to think about what colors and designs they want to use. They also have to think about how they will sew the pieces of their quilts together.

To make a quilt, one piece is often repeated many times to create a design. A quilt piece is a type of tile. Sometimes, many smaller parts are used to make each square. Repeat the squares, and you get a large quilt.

Symmetry can be used to make quilts interesting. You can flip the tiles or rotate them so that their patterns appear in different places. In fact, modern quilters sometimes use computer software to create tessellations. The software shows the quilter how the tiles can be moved around to make different patterns.

M. C. Escher and Beyond

Have you ever seen the artwork done by M. C. Escher (ESH-er)? Escher is famous for using math to create amazing tessellations. At first, he drew designs with simple tessellations. Then he traveled to Spain. There, he saw a castle with bright patterned tiles on the walls and wooden patterns on the ceilings. These patterns used tessellations. He copied the designs. Then he went on to create his own patterns.

As you've seen, tessellations are everywhere. They can be as simple as a four-square flag or as detailed as the designs that Escher created. They can be fun to look at—and fun to make yourself!

one of M. C. Escher's patterns

Glossary

centuries periods of one hundred years

congruent having the same shape and size

gaps areas in which things are missing

mirror to look exactly the same as

mosaic a picture or design made up of pieces, such as stone or tile, arranged onto a surface

overlap to cover one area with another area

polygons closed, flat shapes with three or more straight sides

shades colors that are brighter or darker variations of a given color

symmetry an arrangement of parts so that the parts match on both sides of a center

tiles flat shapes that can be repeated to cover a surface

unit a single thing that makes up part of a whole

Index